CW01500709

LUTON

TRAVEL GUIDE
2024

Explore Luton and Beyond: A Guide to the City and Its Many Attractions. What to See, Do, and Eat

NICOLAS MENDEZ

1

Table of Contents

INTRODUCTION

Salutations, brave voyagers, and salutations from the lively town of Luton! Tucked down in the center of England's Bedfordshire, Luton is a jewel that has yet to be fully appreciated. In my role as your amiable tour guide around this amazing place, I can't wait to share with you all of its mysteries, legends, and wonders in 2024.

About This Travel Guide

Your key to the greatest Luton experience is this guide. It's more than simply a book—carefully curated and infused with local knowledge—it's your travel companion. We have designed an experience that satisfies every interest, from historical sites to delectable cuisine. So let's go off on this journey to discover Luton's captivating tapestry together.

A Few Quick Travel Tips

Here are some brief pointers to ensure that your Luton experience goes well before we get into the details:

Weather Wisdom: The marine climate of Luton is moderate. Because the weather might vary as much as the sights, bring layers.

Currency Matters: The British Pound (£) is the currency used locally. Even though most places take cards, make sure you have enough cash on hand for smaller shops.

Public Transportation is well-functioning in Luton. The Luton rail station, a center for exploration, is located at coordinates (51.8787° N, 0.4200° W).

Local Slang: Although English is the official language, using some local slang may make conversations more interesting. A simple "cheers" will make a big difference!

Let's now explore the core of Luton, beginning with its fascinating past.

Historical Tapestry: **The Unveiling of Luton**

Luton's rich past is told via stories of industrial ingenuity, ethnic variety, and moments of resiliency that weave together like a compelling narrative. The Wardown House Museum (51.8782° N, 0.4123° W) becomes our time machine as we go through the streets. It was once a magnificent home and is now home to displays that bring Luton's history to life.

Explore the Stockwood Discovery Centre (51.8850° N, 0.4422° W), showcasing the town's agricultural heritage via gardens and exhibitions. A fascinating collection of cars and carriages, the Mossman Collection provides a clear picture of Luton's development.

Cultural Hotspots: Where Art and Expression Collide

The Hat Factory Arts Centre (51.8783° N, 0.4169° W) is a must-see for culture vultures. This vibrant venue, which captures the creative energy of Luton, presents a variety of entertainment, including live music and theatrical shows.

Natural Wonders: Luton's Green Oasis

Take a break from the city and enjoy the great outdoors at Stockwood Park (51.8803° N, 0.4399° W). Stroll through beautiful gardens, take in the aromas, and rejuvenate in the tranquil environment.

Accommodation Haven: A Place of Coziness and Charm

Warren Weir (51.8687° N, 0.4094° W), a quaint refuge on the banks of the River Lea, is a great place to rest your feet. It is the ideal starting point for your Luton adventure, offering a hint of elegance and peace.

Culinary Odyssey: Luton's Tastes

Get ready to go on a gustatory adventure through Luton's gastronomic offerings. Enjoy regional specialties at Bear Club (51.8786° N, 0.4176° W), a distinctive dining experience enhanced by creative cuisine and live jazz.

Luton After Dark: An Extravaganza of Nightlife

Experience the vibrant nightlife of Luton as the sun sets. For a night to remember, visit Galaxy Nightclub (51.8789° N, 0.4139° W), which has an electrifying atmosphere and throbbing sounds.

Essential Travel Tips: Easily Navigating Luton

To guarantee smooth navigation, always have the Luton Airport coordinates (51.8742° N, 0.3686° W) close at hand. This main hub makes it easy for you to come and go by connecting you to the town and surrounding areas.

This sneak peek into Luton's charm puts you in a position for an amazing trip. Luton welcomes visitors with wide arms, regardless of their interests in history, the outdoors, or fine cuisine. Now, my lovely passengers, let the journey begin!

As we explore Luton's many facets and lead you through its treasured customs and undiscovered beauties, check back again for further insights. Awaiting you is your Luton journey!

GETTING STARTED

I'm glad you decided to make Luton your next travel destination. Let's go into the specifics of making your travel arrangements so that everything goes as well as possible.

Starting point in Luton Town Center (51.8787° N, 0.4200° W)

1. **Accommodation Selection:** The town center is a good place to stay when deciding where to lay your head. With its convenient location, the Premier Inn Luton Town Centre (51.8783° N, 0.4157° W) is a great starting point for exploring.

2. **Itinerary Crafting:** Create a comprehensive itinerary that highlights Luton's variety. Visit the Luton Indoor Market (51.8783° N, 0.4177° W) first thing in the morning to take in the active vibe of the town.

3. **Cultural Calendar Check:** Look up the local activities calendar before you go on your trip. Often taking place in June, the Hat Festival is a vibrant celebration of Luton's

history as a hat maker. Arranging your trip around these occasions will give your experience a hint of the local flavor.

4. **Weather Wisdom Recap:** Although we discussed this before, let's stress how crucial it is to pack properly. Be ready for a little bit of everything since the weather may be as varied as Luton's attractions.

Best Time to Visit Luton

Luton's charm never goes away, but timing is everything when it comes to seeing it at its best.

1. **Spring (March to May):** Luton's parks and gardens are especially lovely to visit in the springtime when blossoms color the town in shades of pink and white. Beautiful scenery and mild temps combine to create a charming trip.

2. **Summer (June to August):** The Hat Festival often heralds the arrival of pleasant weather and breezy nights. This is the best time of year for festivals, outdoor activities, and eating al fresco.

3. **Autumn (September to November):** Luton becomes a warm-toned canvas as the leaves change color. It's a great

time for walks in parks like Wardown Park (51.8772° N, 0.4122° W) and cultural activities.

4. **Winter (December to February):** Luton has a joyous feel throughout the winter months. Discover the Christmas markets, take in the town's festive lighting, and experience the coziness of the season.

Guide to Transportation

Now that you have your schedule planned and your baggage packed, let's explore Luton's transportation options.

1. **Getting Here**

By Air: Your point of entry to the town is the Lincoln Airport (51.8742° N, 0.3686° W). You will quickly find yourself in the center of Luton thanks to its proximity and well-established transit connections.

By Train: The railroad station in Luton, located at 51.8787° N, 0.4200° W, serves as a key hub for travel to nearby cities and points of interest. For ease, think about purchasing your rail tickets in advance.

2. Getting Around

Walking: Because Luton Town Centre is pedestrian-friendly, you may take your time exploring all of its hidden corners. Put on comfy footwear and enjoy the town as it unfolds under your feet.

Public Transportation: The effective bus system in Luton makes it possible to go to locations outside of the town center. Important bus stops should be noted, such as the one beside Galaxy Centre (51.8789° N, 0.4139° W).

Car Rentals: You might think about hiring a car if you want to go to the picturesque suburbs. Coordinates like those of Enterprise Rent-A-automobile (51.8791° N, 0.3717° W) might be your starting point. Luton provides several automobile rental options.

3. Insider Tip

Cycling in Luton: Riding two wheels is a great way to see Luton for the environmentally concerned tourist. Located at 51.8785° N, 0.4139° W, the Luton Cycle Hub is an excellent place to start your riding travels and offers rental options.

LUTON TRAVEL GUIDE 2024

Equipped with a well-considered itinerary and a grasp of the seasonal subtleties of Luton, you're sure to have a fascinating adventure. Hold this reference close, and start exploring!

EXPLORING LUTON

Luton's historical tapestry is revealed as we go back in time thanks to notable sites that serve as reminders of the town's development.

1. **The museum at Wardown House (51.8782° N, 0.4123° W)**
The Wardown House Museum, a stately home transformed into a time capsule, is where our tour starts. This museum, which is tucked away on Old Bedford Road, takes you through many historical periods in Luton. Every chamber echoes stories of a bygone period, from wartime resiliency to Victorian elegance.

2. **Luton Hoo Mansion**: Travel south to see the splendor of Luton Hoo Mansion (51.8425° N, 0.3769° W). Nestled inside an expansive estate, this home, which doubles as a hotel, has magnificent 18th-century architecture. Its historical charm is enhanced by the peacefulness of the lake and the beautiful gardens.

3. St. Mary's Church (N 51.8792°, W 0.4081°)

Now let's turn our attention to the spiritual history of St. Mary's Church in the center of Luton. This architectural treasure, which dates to the 12th century, is a reflection of many centuries of communal life and devotion. The calm environment encourages reflection despite the activity of the town.

Cultural Hotspot

Beyond its historical foundations, Luton is a vibrant cultural hub. Let's explore the core of creativity and creative expression.

1. The Hat Factory Arts Centre is located at 51.8783° N and 0.4169° W.

Visit the Hat Factory Arts Centre to feel the pulse of modern Luton culture. This vibrant facility, which is situated on Bute Street, presents a variety of events, including live music concerts and innovative theatrical shows. Enter the neighborhood's artistic environment and allow inspiration to envelop you.

2. Culture Trust Luton, located at 51.8789° North and 0.4154° West:
You should visit The Culture Trust Luton if you're looking for an immersive cultural experience. This organization conducts a variety of events, exhibits, and seminars in locations such as the Luton Library Theatre. For an opportunity to interact with Luton's thriving cultural community, check their schedule.

3. **The Bear Club (51.8786° N, 0.4176° W):** Visit The Bear Club on Mill Street for a musical and gastronomic blend of cultures. This cozy jazz club provides delicious food in addition to providing soul-stirring performances. It demonstrates Luton's ability to combine heritage with a modern flare.

Natural Attractions

Beyond its rich history and cultural heritage, Luton is a naturalist's paradise. Let's investigate the verdant havens that adorn the town.

1. **Stockwood Park (51.8803° N, 0.4399° W):** A vast green space that embodies Luton's unspoiled beauty, Stockwood Park attracts visitors. This park offers open areas

for picnics and charming gardens, making it a haven for anyone looking to get away from the city.

2. **The park Leagrave (51.8997° N, 0.4618° W):** Leagrave Park, to the north, provides a tranquil getaway. Take in the peace of the River Lea, stroll through forested regions, and appreciate the beauty of the natural world. For those who like experiences off the beaten route, it's a hidden treasure.

3. **Warden Hills (51.8927° N, 0.4483° W):** This lesser-known natural beauty near Luton has plenty of adventure waiting for you. Explore the wildlife that flourishes in this pristine environment as you hike over the undulating hills and take in the expansive vistas.

Off the Beaten path

Luton has a few surprises in store for the daring travelers looking for lesser-known gems.

1. **The Sensory Garden at Stockwood Discovery Center (51.8850° N, 0.4422° W):** The Sensory Garden is a secret haven located within Stockwood Discovery Center. This garden, which is tucked away from the major displays,

awakens your senses with its relaxing natural noises, tactile textures, and aromatic blossoms.

2. The Maze at Hoo Hill (51.8498° N, 0.3972° W)

Explore the fascinating Hoo Hill Maze, an unusual maze that tests the abilities of both young and elderly. This oddball attraction puts a fun spin on your tour and is located south of Luton.

3. Luton Hoo Estate's Hidden Garden (51.8425° N, 0.3769° W)

Enter the Secret Garden on the Luton Hoo Estate to discover a secluded haven. This private garden, tucked away from the main estate, provides a peaceful haven surrounded by lush vegetation.

As we come to the end of our tour of Luton, keep in mind that the town's charm is found in its secret spots as much as its well-known attractions. Put on your explorer's hat, follow the directions, and let Luton fascinate you as it tells its story. Cheers to your exploration!

NEIGHBORHOODS AND DISTRICTS

Exploring the Heart of Luton

Welcome to the center of Luton, where vibrant districts and residential areas are home to the town's heartbeat. Let's take a tour around the fundamental ideas of Luton.

1. **The Luton Town Centre is located at 51.8787° N and 0.4200° W.**
Start your journey at Luton Town Centre, the center of it all. This thriving, energetic center is home to a wide range of stores, eateries, and cultural centers. Take a stroll along George Street, where street performers and bustling marketplaces create a vibrant scene.

2. **Chapel Street (North: 51.8785°; West: 0.4168°)**
Explore Chapel Street's historic charm, which is adorned with charming stores and restaurants. Visit the artisanal shops and cafés where the scent of freshly brewed coffee calls, like The Roastery Café (email: info@theroasterycafe.com).

LUTON TRAVEL GUIDE 2024

3. **Manchester Street (51.8788° N, 0.4143° W):** Take a stroll down Manchester Street, which has a distinctive aesthetic created by the blend of old and contemporary buildings. Nestled here is The Mall Luton (email: info@themall.co.uk), a shopping heaven with a varied selection of retailers.

4. **Bute Street**: Take a stroll along Bute Street to get a sense of the ethnic variety of Luton (51.8787° N, 0.4181° W). International restaurants like Turkish Kitchen (email: info@turkishkitchenluton.com), where you may have a gastronomic adventure, can be found along this bustling area.

Local Area Hidden Gems

Beneath the main hubbub, Luton's surrounding districts conceal hidden gems. Let's find the undiscovered treasures that give the town personality.

1. **High Town (North 51.8857, West 0.4144)**
Climb to High Town, an elevation area with sweeping views of Luton. Here you'll find independent stores like The Hat Club, a welcoming place that sells distinctive headgear. Send

an email to info@thehatclub.co.uk to secure a place at their Hat Making Workshop.

2. **South Luton (51.8632° N, 0.4128° W):** For a taste of real local flavor, explore the South Luton area. Discover the independent shops on Park Street, such as the well-known Streatlife Café (info@streatlifecafe.co.uk), which serves handmade pastries and has a cozy atmosphere.

3. **Stopsley Village (51.8812° N, 0.3992° W):** Take a stroll around this quaint village that transports you to a bygone era. The Red Lion Pub (info@redlionhotel.net), a historic venue offering traditional British cooking, is not to be missed. For a relaxing time at a pub, make a reservation.

4. **Located at 51.8827° N and 0.4379° W, Crawley Green:**
Welcome to Crawley Green, a quiet neighborhood with a sense of community. Discover The Olive Tree Café, a hidden treasure renowned for its Mediterranean-inspired cuisine (email: info@olivetreecafe.co.uk). A wonderful eating experience is guaranteed with a reservation.

Insider Tips on Exploring Your Neighborhood

Local Events: Look for local festivals and get-togethers on the event calendars. Every area has different cultural events that give your visit a distinct feel.

Walking Tours: Take part in guided walking tours to learn about the communities from the inside out. The enthusiastic local tour guides in Luton infuse the streets with life with their tales and experiences.

Community Markets: Communities such as High Town and Bury Park have regular community markets. These markets, which include everything from locally crafted goods to international cuisine, highlight the lively local culture.

Street Art Trails: Explore South Luton and other districts to find interesting street art. The town serves as a canvas for local painters, who transform walls into colorful works of art.

Keep in mind that every corner you turn, as you navigate Luton's neighborhoods and districts, has a tale to tell and a special experience to provide. Luton's spirit is woven into the fabric of its local communities, whether you're exploring the old streets or enjoying a cup of coffee in a hidden café. So go off the usual track, adhere to the GPS coordinates, and let Luton's communities reveal themselves to you. Cheers to your exploration!

ACCOMMODATION

Reviews and Suggestions for Hotels

Selecting the ideal lodging is essential for an unforgettable trip to Luton. Let's look at a few hotels that enhance your stay with a little regional flair in addition to comfort.

1. **Warren Weir:** Address: Luton Hoo Estate, Luton, LU1 3TQ; 51.8687° N, 0.4094° W

Start your opulent Luton adventure at Warren Weir. This classy hotel (reservations@lutonhoo.com) is tucked away on the Luton Hoo Estate and provides a peaceful haven by the River Lea. Savor lavish accommodations, fine food, and the tranquility of verdant surroundings.

2. **Icon Hotel Luton**: Address: 15 Stuart Street, Luton, LU1 2SA; 51.8782° N, 0.4183° W

Icon Hotel Luton is a great option for a stylish stay in the city. Conveniently located in the center of town, this modern jewel (email: reservations@iconhotelluton.com) blends convenience with modern style. The major attractions of Luton are just a short walk away thanks to its ideal location.

3. **Hampton by Hilton Luton Airport**: 42-50 Kimpton Road, Luton, LU2 0SX (51.8794° N, 0.3767° W)

The proximity of Hampton by Hilton to Luton Airport is ideal for on-the-go travelers. For travelers arriving late or catching an early flight, this well-appointed hotel (email: reservations.lutonairport@hilton.com) offers comfort and convenience.

Budget - Friendly Stays

Luton ensures that cost doesn't sacrifice comfort by offering a range of budget-friendly options. Let's look at some excellent value yet affordable solutions.

1. **Travelodge Luton**: Regent Street, Luton, LU1 5FA is the address (51.8789° N, 0.4206° W).
Without sacrificing quality, Travelodge Luton (email: customer.services@travelodge.co.uk) offers affordable lodging. It's well situated for a low-cost introduction to Luton's attractions, being close to the town center.

2. **Premier Inn Luton Town Centre**: Regent Street, Luton, LU1 5FA is the address (51.8783° N, 0.4157° W).

Budget-conscious tourists may rely on the Premier Inn Luton Town Centre (email: contactus@premierinn.com), which offers cozy accommodations and a convenient location. Savor the ease of having restaurants, shopping, and cultural attractions nearby.

3. **EasyHotel Luton:** 40A Guildford Street, Luton, LU1 2PA; 51.8794° N, 0.4146° W

Affordable lodging in a handy location is offered by easyHotel Luton (email: luton@easyhotel.com) for individuals who choose simplicity without compromising comfort. It's a straightforward choice for tourists on a tight budget who value accessibility.

Unique Accommodation options

Luton has unique alternatives that guarantee an unforgettable stay for people seeking something different from typical hotels.

1. **The Old Palace Lodge**: Church Street, Dunstable, LU5 4RT is the address (51.8789° N, 0.4189° W).

Visit The Old Palace Lodge and embrace history (email: reception@oldpalacelodge.com). This boutique hotel is housed in a historic coaching inn from the 18th century and is close to Dunstable. Take in a mix of contemporary comfort and historic charm.

2. Spending the night on a narrowboat at 51.8896° N and 0.4185° W

Provider: Narrowboat Holidays Beds and Bucks
Take into consideration spending a night aboard a narrowboat for a unique experience. Experience the Grand Union Canal while sleeping under the skies with Beds and Bucks Narrowboat Holidays. Make a reservation inquiry on their website.

3. **Luton Hoo Hotel, Golf & Spa:** Address: The Mansion House, Luton Hoo, Luton, LU1 3TQ; 51.8425° N, 0.3769° W
Luton Hoo Hotel, Golf & Spa (reservations@lutonhoo.com) is more than simply a hotel; it's an experience. Stay at the magnificent Mansion House,

which is encircled by 1,065 acres of lovely parkland. Enjoy spa services, golf, and opulence for a really elegant getaway.

Luxurious lodging, affordable comfort, or an exclusive experience are all available in Luton, where a wide range of lodging options are available to accommodate every taste. Make an informed decision, and allow your residence to add to the entire charm of your Luton experience. Enjoy your stay!

DINING AND NIGHTLIFE

Culinary Delights in Luton

The gastronomic landscape of Luton is a patchwork of tastes, mirroring the town's multifarious cultural fabric. Together, let's explore the culinary marvels that Luton has to offer.

1. **Bianco Nero, located at 51.8802° N and 0.4139° W:** 25–27 Church Street, Luton, LU1 3AJ is the address.

Bianco Nero, a little Italian restaurant nestled away on Church Street (email: info@bianconero.co.uk), is a great place to start your culinary trip. It's a sanctuary for pasta, pizza, and Italian food enthusiasts with its cozy atmosphere and genuine delicacies.

2. **Meimo, located at 51.8795° N and 0.4143° W:** Address: LU1 2QH, 70 Wellington Street, Luton

Travel to Meimo, a hidden treasure with a focus on Lebanese food. Enjoy mezes, shawarma, and falafel to fully experience the rich tastes of the Middle East. Please contact info@meimorestaurant.com to make bookings.

3. The Brache (51.8995° N, 0.4281° W)

Osborne Road, Luton, LU1 3HJ is the address.

Visit The Brache (email: hello@thebrache.co.uk) for modern British food in a chic Osborne Road location. This restaurant has a varied cuisine made with regional products, ranging from substantial breakfasts to sophisticated entrees.

Neighborhood Cafés and Restaurants

Where Luton's unique culinary character comes through is in its local restaurants. Let's investigate a few well-liked locations that encapsulate the spirit of the neighborhood.

1. Located at 51.8785° N and 0.4172° W, Elles Baguettes:

3 Church Street, Luton, LU1 3AJ is the address.

Treat your taste buds to a wonderful sandwich and freshly baked products at Elles Baguettes, a little café. In the center of Luton, this place (email: info@ellesbaguettes.co.uk) provides the ideal balance of comfort and taste.

2. **Kobeda Palace is located at 51.8805° N and 0.4276° W.**

174 Dunstable Road, Luton, LU1 1EW is the address.

For a sample of the Afghan food that has won over the hearts of the people, visit Kobeda Palace. Known for its flavorful meals and tender kebabs, this restaurant (info@kobedapalace.com) offers a genuine gastronomic experience.

3. **51.8786° N, 0.4176° W is the Bear Club Café:**

Mill Yard, Mill Street, Luton, LU1 2NA is the address.

Enjoy a great range of coffees and pastries at The Bear Club Café, which is an extension of the jazz club. Sip your favorite beer and take in the live music and artsy atmosphere.

Entertainment & Scenes from Nightlife

Luton becomes a colorful canvas of nightlife and excitement once the sun sets. Let's investigate the sceneries that illuminate the town at night.

1. **Galaxy Nightclub: located at 51.8789° N and 0.4139° W.**

31–35 Mill Street, Luton, LU1 2NA is the address.

Enter Galaxy Nightclub and experience the upbeat music—a popular destination for anybody looking for a fun night out. Enjoy a night of dancing to a variety of musical genres. For VIP bookings, send an email to vip@galaxyluton.co.uk.

2. **51.8787° N, 0.4123° W) is The Edge.**

84 Park Street, Luton, LU1 3ET is the address.

Explore the alternative culture at The Edge, a place well-known for its varied events and live music. To inquire about future performances and events, send an email to info@theedgevenue.co.uk.

3. **White House coordinates: 51.8775° N, 0.4147° W**

4A Windmill Lane, Luton, LU1 3XJ is the address.

Visit The White House, a welcoming gastropub, for a relaxed evening. Savor handmade brews, traditional mixed drinks, and live acoustic shows. Send an email to bookings@thewhitehouseluton.co.uk to make a table reservation.

Must-Try Dishes

Many different meals in Luton's culinary scene invite foodies to experience the town's delights. To enhance your culinary journey, consider trying these foods that are a must:

1. **Luton Hotpot:** A regional specialty consisting of a delicious broth, root vegetables, and savory meat. This rich meal, frequently available in classic British pubs like The Red Lion Pub (see Unique Accommodation Options), is a great way to experience comfort on a plate.

2. **Bedfordshire Clanger:** This regional delicacy will sate your demands for both sweet and savory foods. The Bedfordshire Clanger has two fillings: sweet fruit on one end and meat on the other. Find this delicious delicacy in markets and bakeries in the area.

3. **Kobeda Kebab**: Savor the mouthwatering tastes of this neighborhood staple. Perfectly cooked on the grill, these skewers go well with savory sauces and fragrant rice. For

traditional cooking, Kobeda Palace (see Local Restaurants and Cafés) is highly recommended.

Food Markets and Street food

Visit the bustling street food scene and neighborhood markets for a taste of Luton's diverse gastronomic offerings on the go.

1. Located at 51.8786° N and 0.4128° W, Luton International Carnival Food Village:
Address: Luton's Wardown Park

Savor an international feast in the Food Village during the Luton International Carnival. This lively market honors the town's diversity of cultures with offerings ranging from Asian street cuisine to Caribbean jerk chicken.

2. Location: 51.8783° N, 0.4177° W, Luton Indoor Market:
The Market Hall, Luton, LU1 2TA is the address.

Explore the Luton Indoor Market, the center of the city's gastronomic culture. Discover the many different cuisines available at the vendors, including freshly baked products and aromatic spices.

Dietary Options and Expertise

To ensure that everyone can enjoy the town's gastronomic delights, Luton welcomes a variety of dietary preferences. The following establishments accommodate certain dietary requirements:

1. **Olive Tree Café: located at 51.8812° North and 0.3992° West.**
10 Church Street, Luton, LU1 3JS is the address.

The Olive Tree Café is a paradise for vegans and vegetarians. This place (info@olivetreecafe.co.uk) specializes in cuisine that is inspired by the Mediterranean region, with an emphasis on using fresh and plant-based products.

2. **Gourmet Grill: located at 51.8788° N and 0.4126° W.**
95 Park Street, Luton, LU1 3HG is the address.

Those who like halal cuisine will enjoy what Gourmet Grill has to offer. This place serves halal food and is well-known for its succulent burgers and grilled treats.

3. The Bakery Without Gluten (51.8818° N, 0.4213° W):

12 Chapel Street, Luton, LU1 2SE is the address.

This Chapel Street bakery is committed to serving gluten-free baked goods. Savory sweets and freshly baked goods without sacrificing your dietary requirements.

Luton offers a vibrant blend of cuisine, entertainment, and cultures in its eating and nightlife scenes. The town welcomes you to revel in its rich gastronomic tapestry, whether you're tasting regional cuisine, discovering secret cafés, dancing the night away, or finding unusual street food. So go off to explore Luton's cuisine by following the coordinates, booking your tables, and seeing it all come to life. Cheers to a night full of amazing encounters and bon appétit!

SHOPPING IN LUTON

Retail Therapy: Top Places to Shop

From vibrant markets to cutting-edge shopping malls, Luton has a lot to offer shoppers. Let's investigate the top stores that provide everything for every taste and choice.

1. The Mall Luton: 37 George Street, Luton, LU1 2AZ (51.8788° N, 0.4143° W)

Start your shopping adventure at The Mall Luton, a major retail center with a wide variety of shops, from niche boutiques to high-street names. This shopping wonderland (email: info@themall.co.uk) has everything you need, from gadgets to clothes.

2. George Street: Luton, George Street (51.8789° N, 0.4139° W)

Explore George Street, which has a unique blend of boutiques, cafés, and stores. Discover distinctive treasures by perusing carefully chosen vintage clothing in independent shops like Vintage Darling (email: info@vintagedarling.co.uk).

3. Luton Indoor Market: Address: The Market Hall, Luton, LU1 2TA; 51.8783° N, 0.4177° W

Take in the energetic ambiance of Luton Indoor Market. Look around the booths offering anything from handmade goods to fresh veggies. It's the ideal location to find handcrafted treasures and hidden jewels in the area.

4. The Hat District: Hat House, 32–44 Guildford Street, Luton, LU1 2NR; 51.8818° N, 0.4213° W

At The Hat District, a center for the arts and culture, unleash your creative side. Look around galleries and art studios; you may find original pieces of art to bring home as a one-of-a-kind memento.

Unique Souvenirs to Bring Home

Luton provides a selection of unique mementos that encapsulate the spirit of the community. Consider taking home one of these unusual objects as a keepsake from your trip:

1. **The Luton Hat**

Locate Luton Hat Works at 51.8797° N and 0.4205° W.

Embrace Luton's illustrious history of creating hats by taking one home. Explore the history of hat-making and buy a fashionable hat to remember your visit to Luton Hat Works, a museum and cultural center.

2. **Handicraft Jewelry**

The Arches Craft Hub is located at 51.8783° N, 0.4224° W.

Discover the Arches Craft Hub, a creative hub that helps out regional makers. Consider purchasing jewelry that is created and showcases the beauty and skill of Luton's gifted artisans.

3. **Official Luton Town FC Apparel**

The Luton Town FC Club Shop can be found at 51.8895° N, 0.4199° W.

Get some Luton Town FC souvenirs from the club store if you're a sports fan. Whether it's a collectible jersey, scarf, or other item, it's a great way to become involved with the town's sports culture.

4. **Luton Craft Beer**

Where to Find: Different Locations of Craft Beer Shops Think about carrying a taste of Luton home with you in the form of artisan brews if you like regional tastes. Discover the town's brewing culture by visiting the area breweries or specialist craft beer stores, where you may find an assortment of distinctive beers.

Tips for a Smooth Shopping Experience

Local Markets: Take advantage of the chance to visit nearby markets such as Bury Park Market and Luton Indoor Market. These busy centers are veritable gold mines of unusual finds and genuine local experiences.

Independent shops: Explore independent shops on Luton's picturesque streets by venturing outside of large retail malls. These shops often provide hand-selected goods and individualized attention.

Craft Hubs & Artisanal Workshops: These are places where you may meet local artists and buy handcrafted items. Keep a watch out for them. One excellent example that provides a window into Luton's creative environment is the Arches Craft Hub.

Seasonal Markets and Events: For information on seasonal markets and special events, see the local events calendar. These events often include a wide variety of merchants, offering a unique shopping opportunity.

Let your senses lead you through the lively streets and marketplaces as you explore Luton's retail environment. Luton welcomes you to explore and take part in a great shopping journey, whether you're looking for trendy bargains, unusual gifts, or a taste of local workmanship. Cheers to your shopping!

OUTDOOR ACTIVITIES

Parks and Recreation Areas

Luton extends an invitation to nature lovers to discover its parks and recreational spaces. The town offers a range of outdoor settings to suit every desire, whether you're looking for peace or an energetic adventure.

1. Wardown Park: Old Bedford Road, Luton, LU2 7HA is the address (51.8778° N, 0.4148° W).

Start exploring the great outdoors in Wardown Park, a vast verdant haven by the River Lea. This park is great for boat trips on the lake, picnics, and strolls. Bring your tennis rackets to the courts or take the family to the play area for an exciting day.

2. Stockwood Park: London Road, Luton, LU1 4LX; address: 51.8803° N, 0.4399° W

Experience the splendor of Stockwood Park, which combines open areas, historical displays, and beautiful gardens. Stroll around the Sensory Garden at your leisure, visit the Stockwood Discovery Center, or just relax in the tranquil surroundings.

3. Leagrave Park: Marsh Road, Luton, LU3 2NL; 51.8997° N, 0.4618° W

Take a break and visit Leagrave Park, a hidden treasure in Luton's northern region. Explore the pathways along the River Lea, stroll through forested regions, and take in the tranquil environment that characterizes this natural hideaway.

4. Houghton Hall Park: Parkside Drive, Houghton Regis, LU5 5QN; address: 51.8965° N, 0.4034° W

Go a little way beyond Luton to Houghton Hall Park, a beautiful green area including both open fields and forests. With its play area, natural habitats, and café for a post-adventure treat, the park is perfect for family trips.

Luton Adventure Sports

Luton has a variety of exhilarating outdoor activities that are sure to raise your heart rate for adventure seekers and thrill-lovers.

1. The XC: 34–38 Junction 10 Business Park, Dallow Road, Luton, LU1 1TR; Address: 51.8892° N, 0.4022° W

Immerse yourself in adventure in the thrilling sports and recreation facility, The XC. Take on the thrill of indoor skiing and snowboarding, ride the BMX track, or test your climbing prowess on the indoor climbing wall. Email info@thexc.co.uk to make reservations.

2. Go Ape at Warden Hills: Warden Hill Road, Luton, LU2 7AE is the address (51.8927° N, 0.4483° W).

At Go Ape, an adventure course tucked away in the Warden Hills, swing through the trees. For an exhilarating day out, conquer zip lines, Tarzan swings, and rope bridges. For an exhilarating outdoor adventure, book via their website.

3. Outdoor Activities at Luton Hoo Estate (51.8425° N, 0.3769° W): Luton Hoo Estate, LU1 3TQ is the address.

Discover the expansive Luton Hoo Estate, which is a haven for outdoor enthusiasts. Offering a variety of sports in a lovely environment, the estate provides archery and clay pigeon shooting. The estate's outdoor activities staff may be reached at outdooractivities@lutonhoo.com for reservations.

4. River Lea Kayaking (Various Locations): Provider: Trail Canoe

Canoe along the River Lea and paddle your way through adventure. Canoe Trail provides guided kayaking excursions so you may enjoy the beautiful rivers. Go to their website for information and bookings.

Tips For Outdoor Exploration

Seasonal Considerations: Before scheduling any outside activities, check the weather and seasonal options. Seasonality may apply to certain activities, and the weather may affect your whole experience.

Equipment Rental: Find out about your alternatives for renting equipment if you're trying out adventure sports. Numerous companies, including Canoe Trail and Go Ape, rent out equipment, so you can be sure you have all you need for a fun and safe adventure.

Guided Tours: If you want a more immersive experience, think about going on a guided tour. The history, importance, and natural beauty of the outdoor regions you visit may be imparted by local guides.

Safety First: Put safety first by adhering to rules and directions, particularly while participating in adventure sports. Choose beginner-friendly alternatives and make sure you're with knowledgeable advisors if you're new to the activity.

The outdoor experiences available in Luton provide the ideal ratio of peace and thrill. The town welcomes you to enjoy the great outdoors, whether you're looking for an adrenaline rush from adventure sports or a relaxing day in the parks. Now gather your belongings, verify the GPS coordinates, and enjoy the unspoiled beauty of Luton. Happy voyaging!

CULTURAL EXPERIENCES

Museums and Galleries

Explore Luton's museums and galleries to learn more about its unique cultural tapestry. These cultural treasures provide an engrossing look into the history, traditions, and artwork of the town.

1. **Wardown House, Museum, and Gallery: Old Bedford Road, Luton, LU2 7HA is the address (51.8778° N, 0.4148° W).**

Experience a historical voyage at Wardown House, Museum, and Gallery. A fascinating collection spanning the history of Luton is housed in this Victorian home. View displays on the town's development, fashion, and local enterprises. Reach out to info@lutonculture.com for guided tours.

2. **The Hat Works: 14-16 Guildford Street, Luton, LU1 2NR; 51.8797° N, 0.4205° W**

Visit The Hat Works to get fully immersed in Luton's hat-making history. This cultural center provides information about the history and workmanship of the town's millinery. Admire the variety of hats in the collection and learn about the craftsmanship that goes into these classic fashion items.

3. **The Culture Trust Luton: Address: Multiple Locations (51.8787° N, 0.4183° W)**

The Luton Library Theatre and the Stockwood Discovery Centre are only two of the cultural institutions that are part of the Culture Trust Luton. For information on forthcoming shows, concerts, and other events that highlight the thriving arts and cultural sector, see the trust's website.

Festivals and Events

Numerous festivals and events bring Luton to life, celebrating its rich cultural diversity and sense of community. Participate in the celebrations and make treasured memories while you're there.

1. **Luton International Carnival (Many Locations): carnival@luton.gov.uk is the email address.**

Take in the energy of one of Europe's biggest one-day carnivals, the Luton International Carnival. Admire the vibrant procession, groove to international music, and savor international food in the Food Village. Contact the carnival organizers for participation and event information.

2. Luton Live (Many Sites): Send an email to info@lutonbid.org

Luton Live is a series of events that provide entertainment, dancing, and music to the town's streets. These events include live music and street performances by the town's creative talent. Please email info@lutonbid.org to reach Luton BID with any changes or schedules.

3. Luton Lights (Multiple Locations): Send an email to info@lutonbid.org.

Come celebrate the start of the holiday season at the Luton Lights Switch-On. Come celebrate the town's lighting with the locals as they enjoy beautiful lights, joyous entertainment, and a festive atmosphere. Contact Luton BID at info@lutonbid.org for event information.

Annual Celebrations

Luton's yearly festivals encapsulate the spirit of community and ethnic variety. Take part in these joyous occasions to establish a stronger bond with the community.

1. Saint Patrick's Day Events (Multiple Locations): Send an email to events@luton.gov.uk.

Take in the sights and sounds of Ireland on St. Patrick's Day in Luton. Savor the vibrant environment, traditional music, and dancing at many spots across the town. Get in touch with the event planners at events@luton.gov.uk for further information.

2. Diwali Events (Multiple Venues): Send an email to info@lutonbid.org

Take in the splendor of Diwali, the Festival of Lights, with the lively activities held in Luton. Take part in the cultural celebrations, which will include traditional shows, mouth watering Indian food, and the lighting of diyas (oil lights). Get in touch with Luton BID at info@lutonbid.org for event updates.

3. **Luton Carnival Arts Weekend: carnival@luton.gov.uk is the email address to send inquiries.**

Take advantage of Luton Carnival Arts Weekend to explore the world of carnival arts. Take part in classes, see artistic exhibits, and collaborate with the community on a range of artistic projects. Get in touch with the carnival organizers at carnival@luton.gov.uk for information on participation and the event.

Cultural Festivals

The cultural events in Luton provide an insight into the town's varied history, customs, and creative manifestations. Take part in these enlightening activities that honor the community's ethnic fabric.

1. **Luton Mela (Many Locations):** info@lutonmela.co.uk is the email address.

Visit the Luton Mela, a lively event with dance, music, and delectable food, to celebrate South Asian culture. Take part in the celebrations, visit market booths, and enjoy a day full of cultural activities. Contact info@lutonmela.co.uk to reach the organizers for participation and event details.

2. **Luton Irish Forum Festival:** info@lutonirishforum.org is the email address to contact.

The Luton Irish Forum Festival uses dance, music, and cultural exhibits to highlight the diversity of Irish culture. Take part in traditional Irish activities and performances that honor the contributions made by the Irish community of Luton. Contact the Luton Irish Forum at info@lutonirishforum.org for information on the event.

3. **Luton International Film Festival** (Many Locations): [info@lutonfilm.com] is the email address.

Visit the Luton International Film Festival to find hidden treasures in international film. Watch films that make you think, go to screenings and conversations, and appreciate the craft of filmmaking. You may email the organizers at info@lutonfilm.com with questions or updates about the event.

Sporting Events

Luton has a variety of thrilling sporting events for fans of sports that highlight the town's love of athletics and camaraderie.

1. **Playoff games for Luton Town FC** (51.8895° N, 0.4199° W):

Kenilworth Road Stadium, 1 Maple Road, Luton, LU4 8AW is the address.
At the home games of Luton Town FC, support the Hatters. Take in the electrifying ambiance of Kenilworth Road Stadium while watching exhilarating football matches. Go to the official club website to reserve tickets and see the schedule of matches.

2. **Love Luton Half Marathon**: Send an email to events@love-luton.co.uk (several locations).

For the Love Luton Half Marathon, put on your running shoes. Come participate in this community-focused event that encourages fitness and well-being with people from all around the area and beyond. Contact the event organizers at events@love-luton.co.uk for registration information and event specifics.

3. **Luton Hoo Estate Golf:** Address: Luton Hoo Estate, Luton, LU1 3TQ; 51.8425° N, 0.3769° W

Come to the Luton Hoo Estate to enjoy the elegance of golf. At this historic estate, tee off among gorgeous scenery and enjoy a game of golf. Get in touch with the Luton Hoo Estate Golf Club with any questions or to schedule a tee time.

Seasonal Recommendations

With these suggestions catered to the shifting scenery and celebrations, discover the beauty of Luton all year round.

1. **Spring Blossoms in Stockwood Park**: London Road, Luton, LU1 4LX is the address.

Celebrate the coming of spring by taking a tour of Stockwood Park's blooming gardens. See the brilliant hues of flowers in bloom; this is the perfect time of year for a family picnic or a leisurely walk.

2. **Wardown Park Summer Evenings**: Old Bedford Road, Luton, LU2 7HA

Take advantage of the summer's longer daylight hours by visiting Wardown Park in the evening. Take in the captivating atmosphere as the sun sets over the park by attending outdoor activities like concerts or theatrical shows.

3. **Leagrave Park's Autumnal Colors**:
Marsh Road, Luton, LU3 2NL is the address.

At Leagrave Park, the leaves turn into a tapestry of reds, yellows, and oranges, embracing the warmth of fall. Enjoy the breathtaking scenery as you stroll along the riverbanks and take in the beauty of the changing seasons.

4. **The XC's Winter Wonderland**: 34–38 Junction 10 Business Park, Dallow Road, Luton, LU1 1TR
Indulge in the holiday cheer at The XC this winter. Take part in indoor winter sports like skiing and climbing to have a winter wonderland journey and a wonderful getaway from the weather.

The cultural experiences of Luton are a colorful tapestry woven with festivals, festivities, art, and history. Luton wants you to fully immerse yourself in its rich cultural legacy, whether you're touring museums, enjoying a carnival, or supporting your favorite football club. So plan your vacation, put this vibrant town on your calendar, and watch as the cultural adventure takes you there.

PRACTICAL INFORMATION

Travel Essentials

By taking into account these travel necessities, you may ensure a smooth and pleasurable trip to Luton.

1. **Transportation**

Airport: The main air entrance to the town is Luton Airport (51.8740° N, 0.3682° W), for those coming by air. Decide whether you want to use a cab, shuttle, or public transportation for your transfer from the airport.

Railway: Luton has excellent rail connections. An important hub is the Luton Railway Station (51.8787° N, 0.4146° W). Examine rail timetables and make appropriate travel plans.

2. **Accommodation**

Hotels: Look into several lodging choices according to your tastes. Among the well-known lodgings is the Icon Hotel Luton (51.8791° N, 0.4115° W).

15 Stuart Street, Luton, LU1 2SA is the address.

Holiday Inn Luton South: London Road, Markyate, St Albans, AL3 8HH is the address (51.8562° N, 0.4341° W). reservations@hilutonsouth.com is the reservation email.

3. **Currency and Clothing**

Currency Exchange: Visit your neighborhood bank or currency exchange office to swap currencies.
ATMs: For easy access to cash withdrawals, ATMs are extensively distributed.

4. **Weather and Clothing**

Check the Forecast: Recognize the weather before planning your trip. Luton has typical British weather, so bring appropriate clothing.
Layers and adaptable apparel will help you adjust to shifting weather conditions.

5. **Local transportation**
Buses: The bus system in Luton is rather large. Learn the routes and timetables so that you may commute locally conveniently.

Taxis: If you need transportation on demand, taxis are easily accessible.

6. Power Adapters

UK normal: The power outlets used by Luton are normal UK ones. Make sure you have the right power adapters with you for your electronics.

7. Language

English: The most often spoken language is English. Phrases in basic English might be useful for conversation.

Local Customs and Etiquette

Gaining an understanding of Luton's traditions and etiquette will improve your cultural experience there. Here are some pointers for smoothly navigating social situations.

1. Greetings

Handshakes: A traditional way to welcome someone is with a solid handshake. Keep your eyes open while extending a welcome.

2. Politeness

"Please" and "Thank You": Being courteous is important. Say "thank you" and "please" to others.

3. Queuing

British Queuing: Observe the custom of standing in line politely, as part of the British tradition.

4. Tipping

Restaurants: If the service fee is not included, tipping in the range of 10% to 15% is common.
Taxis: Always round up your fare in a cab.

5. Punctuality

Timekeeping: Being on time is highly valued. Be prompt for meetings and appointments.

6. Conduct in Public

Public Spaces: Keep a certain degree of silence in waiting rooms and on public transportation.

Littering: To keep public areas tidy, dispose of waste in the appropriate containers.

7. Privacy

Recognize Privacy: Give people their space and refrain from asking invasive inquiries.

8. Dress code

Smart Casual: Although Luton is a varied community, most venues allow smart casual clothing.

Contacts for Emergencies

To guarantee a prompt response in an emergency, it is essential to have the appropriate contact information on hand.

1. Emergency Services

In an emergency, dial 999 for police, fire, or ambulance help.

2. **Medical Support**:

National Health Service (NHS): For non-emergency medical advice, call 111 of the NHS.

3. **Community Hospitals**

The address of the Luton and Dunstable University Hospital is Lewsey Road, Luton, LU4 0DZ (51.8913° N, 0.4466° W).
In an emergency, dial 999 to send an ambulance.

4. **Misplaced or Stolen Goods**

Contact

Police Station: Notify the neighborhood police station of any lost or stolen property.
The address of the Luton Police Station is Buxton Road, Luton, LU1 1SA (51.8782° N, 0.4115° W).

5. **Consular Services**
Consulates and Embassies: in the event of an emergency or misplaced papers, contact the embassy or consulate of your nation.

6. **Travel Assistance**

Information about Local Tourism (51.8790° N, 0.4175° W):
St George's Square, Luton, LU1 2AZ is the address.
contact@visitluton.org via email

A seamless and pleasurable trip to Luton is ensured by
navigating practical issues and comprehending local
traditions. These must-have travel items, manners advice,
and emergency numbers will set you up for a rewarding stay
in this energetic town.

DAY TRIPS FROM LUTON

Excursions to Nearby Destinations

Though Luton has a lot to offer, think about expanding your journey by taking day visits to neighboring places. Discover the quaint surroundings for a variety of sights to see and unique experiences.

1. **St. Albans** (51.7519° N, 0.3333° W): About 10 miles separate it from Luton.
The address of St. Albans Cathedral is Sumpter Yard, St. Albans, AL1 1BY.

Discover the stunning St. Albans Cathedral, a historical landmark with a rich past spanning many centuries. Admire the magnificent Gothic architecture, explore the wall paintings from the Middle Ages, and climb the tower to get sweeping views.

Verulamium Park

St Michael's Street, St Albans, AL3 4SW is the address.

Take it easy at Verulamium Park, which is centered on the Roman city of Verulamium's remains. Savor the calm lakes and verdant areas, and learn about Roman history by visiting the Verulamium Museum.

St. Albans City Center shopping

The city core of St. Albans has a mix of independent shops and high-street retailers. Discover boutique shopping in Christopher Place and indulge in regional food in the bustling marketplace.

2. **Whipsnade Zoo:** About nine miles from Luton (51.8342° N, 0.5975° W)

Whipsnade Zoo ZSL
Address: LU6 2LF, Dunstable

Visit ZSL Whipsnade Zoo, one of the biggest zoos in the UK, and go on a wildlife adventure. See a wide variety of animals, including lions and elephants, and take in informative seminars and exhibits.

Safari Experience

Drive through the 'Passage through Asia' exhibit, one of the zoo's unique safari experiences. See deer, rhinos, and other Asian creatures in an expansive, unspoiled environment.

Family-Friendly Activities

Family-friendly attractions at Whipsnade Zoo include playgrounds, a steam train, and even the opportunity to spend the night at the Lookout Lodge for a fully immersive experience.

3. The Gardens and Abbey at Woburn (51.9839° N, 0.5979° W):

The distance is around fifteen miles from Luton.

Woburn Abbey
Address: MK17 9WA, Woburn

Discover the venerable Woburn Abbey, a magnificent residence situated on a 3,000-acre estate. Explore lavish chambers, and vast artwork collections, and meander through exquisitely designed gardens.

Deer park Safari

Tour the Woburn Abbey Deer Park on a deer park safari. Take in the breathtaking scenery and tranquility of seeing herds of deer wandering freely in their natural environment.

Woburn Safari Park: Woburn, MK17 9QN; 51.9857° N, 0.6067° W

The safari park, which is next to Woburn Abbey, offers an immersive experience with its animal displays. Savor several wildlife encounters, the Road Safari, and the Foot Safari.

4. **Hitchin Lavender: About ten miles from Luton (51.9791° N, 0.2780° W).**

Farm Hitchin Lavender
Cadwell Farm, Ickleford, Hitchin, SG5 3UA is the address.

Visit Hitchin Lavender Farm and lose yourself in a sea of lavender. Take beautiful pictures, stroll through aromatic lavender fields, and even harvest your lavender to bring home.

Sunflower Fields (Seasonal)

Hitchin Lavender Farm also has colorful sunflower fields in the summer. Take in the gorgeous surroundings and the golden tones of the sunflowers.

Lavender Products

Explore a variety of lavender-infused items in the farm store, such as oils and sachets, so you may carry the calming scent of lavender with you wherever you go.

Guided Tour and Activities

Make the most of your day excursions by adding guided tours and activities, which provide thoughtful discovery and well-chosen experiences.

1. Dunstable Downs: around 8 miles from Luton (51.8512° N, 0.5627° W)

Guided Walks

Take guided treks in the picturesque Chiltern Hills' Dunstable Downs. Experienced guides can tell you everything about the history, flora, and animals of the chalk grasslands.

Flying a kite

Use the areas that are open to fly kites. The expansive scenery and moderate incline of Dunstable Downs make it the perfect place to engage in this traditional outdoor sport.

2. **51.7731° N, 0.9719° W, or the Chiltern Hills**

Distance from Luton: Ten to fifteen miles away from various entry locations

Cycling Tours in the Countryside

Take bicycle excursions across the scenic Chiltern Hills in the countryside. Numerous routes accommodate varying degrees of expertise, offering a pleasurable means of seeing the area's natural splendor.

Tours of Chiltern Wineries

Explore the nearby wineries and vineyards tucked away in the Chiltern Hills. Take part in guided excursions to taste local wines and see how they are made.

3. Harpenden Common (51.8192° N, 0.3526° W)

Five miles or so separate Luton from this location.

Bird Watching Tours

For birdwatchers, Harpenden Common is a paradise. To see a range of bird species in their native environment, sign up for guided bird-watching trips.

Workshops on Nature Photography

Take advantage of wildlife photography seminars to capture the splendor of Harpenden Common. Learn how to take pictures of plants, animals, and landscapes with the help of knowledgeable teachers.

Tips for Day Trips

Check Opening Hours: Make sure you know when the attractions are open and adjust your visit schedule appropriately.

Seasonal Considerations: Certain activities are exclusive to certain seasons, such as sunflower fields and lavender picking. To get the best experiences, check the seasons.

Reserve Guided Tours in Advance: To guarantee a well-organized experience and to guarantee your position on guided tours and activities, it is advisable to reserve your spot in advance.

Local Transportation: To make your vacation go more smoothly, be aware of your alternatives for local transportation for day excursions, whether it be by bus, rail, or automobile.

Because of its closeness to interesting places, Luton offers a great chance for stimulating day excursions. Every trip guarantees a distinctive and unforgettable experience, whether you're taking in the breathtaking countryside, interacting with animals, or seeing historical places. Arrange your day excursions from Luton and see the varied splendor around this vibrant town.

LOCAL INSIGHT : Interviews with Locals

Learn insightful things about Luton from the people that live there. Let's get started by speaking with locals who will offer their best places to visit, hidden treasures, and advice for an amazing trip.

1. Jane, Independent Bookstore Owner of "The Book Nook":

51.8783° N, 0.4153° W is the location.
1A George Street, Luton, LU1 2AA is the address.

Q: Why is "The Book Nook" a must-go-to place in Luton?

Jane: "The Book Nook is a literary sanctuary, not merely a bookshop. We arrange author events, maintain a well-curated selection of books, and provide a welcoming environment. Locals gather there because they have a passion for storytelling in common."

Q: Any recommendations for book lovers visiting Luton?

Jane: "Find writings that have been influenced by Luton by perusing our 'Local Authors' section. Don't miss our author meet-ups and book clubs—they're a great opportunity to learn about the local literary scene."

2. Mark, the chef of the restaurant "Flavors of Luton":

Location: 0.4136° W, 51.8770° N
22 Guildford Street, Luton, LU1 2NR is the address.
reservations@FlavorsoFluton.com via email

Q: What culinary adventures best characterize the food scene in Luton?

Mark: "The food scene in Luxembourg is a mash-up. You have to sample the regional specialties, such as the typical bread Luton Rye, and sample the variety of tastes available at our food markets. We take great pride in the many inspirations we have.

Q: Are there any specialties at "Flavors of Luton"?

Mark: "Our 'Luton Fusion Platter' embodies the spirit of our multicultural neighborhood. It offers bite-sized snacks influenced by the town's many culinary traditions. A gourmet adventure presented on a dish!"

3. Sarah, the Stockwood Discovery Center's curator:

51.8843° N, 0.4044° W is the location.
Luton, LU1 4LX; London Road;
info@stockwooddiscoverycentre.com

Q: What distinguishes Stockwood Discovery Centre as a distinct cultural attraction?

Sarah: "Luton's past is buried deep in Stockwood. It's a reflection of our history, from the lovely gardens to the local industry displays. For people of all ages, the Discovery Galleries provide engaging experiences."

Q: Any insider tips for visitors exploring Stockwood?

Sarah: "Discover hidden tales on our guided garden excursions. Take advantage of the 'Living History' events, which bring history to life. Every part of this area has a story to tell."

Insider Tips for an Exciting Journey

Get insider advice from residents to improve your time in Luton. From lesser-known landmarks to useful guidance, these insights guarantee an unforgettable journey.

1. 51.8714° N, 0.4150° W is **Jake's Photography Hideout:**

Email: jakesphotohideout@gmail.com; Location: Wardown Park, Luton

Tip from jake

Jake: "Go to the less well-known locations along the river for the greatest views of Wardown Park. It's a photographer's paradise. I can even provide you with a map of my top picture spots if you contact me."

2. **Lucy's Undiscovered Treasure Café** (54.1777° N, 4.4191° W).

5 Chapel Street, Luton, LU1 2SE is the address. Lucy'shiddengemcafe@gmail.com is her email.

Tip from Lucy

Lucy: "Leave the throng at my hidden Chapel Street café. A cozy little shop with the greatest pastries baked in-house. I'll make sure to arrange a window seat for you if you email me in advance."

3. **Luton Nature Walks with Mike** (51.8788° N, 0.4314° W):

Location: All around Luton on several nature paths MikesNatureWalks@gmail.com is his email.

Tip from Mike

Mike: "Take one of my guided nature walks to discover Luton's natural splendor. Every walk is different, whether it's along the Lea River or via the undiscovered paths close to Stopsley. Send me an email to sign up for the next expedition."

4. **Emily's Artisan Workshop** is located at 51.8802° N and 0.4127° W.

Address: LU1 2NA, 18 Mill Street, Luton
Emily's Art Workshop

Tip from Emily

Emily: "Come inside my Mill Street workshop and let your imagination run wild. An artisan's paradise with anything from paintings to ceramics. I'll customize a hands-on experience for your creative journey if you email me in advance."

Final Thought

Beyond its tourist attractions, Luton is a charming town full of people, stories, and delicious food. Make use of the insider knowledge provided by individuals who live in Luton to interact with locals, sample delicious hidden cuisine, and discover the town's rich cultural heritage. The tales you gather along the road are just as important to your trip as the locations you see.

LUTON FOR EVERY SEASON

1) Springtime Splendors

Luton comes alive in the springtime, a kaleidoscope of colorful flowers and foliage. Discover Luton's captivating splendor this season with these enjoyable activities.

Stockwood Park Gardens: The location is 51.8843° N and 0.4044° W.

London Road, Luton, LU1 4LX is the address. Welcome springtime at Stockwood Park Gardens. Explore the flower beds that are in full bloom, take in the breathtaking view of the cherry blossoms, and relax in this peaceful botanical retreat. Remember to check out the local history exhibits in the Discovery Center.

Pro Tip: Visit in the early morning when the gardens are touched by the gentle light of dawn for a peaceful experience.

Wardown Park; coordinates: 51.8777° N, 0.4179° W
Old Bedford Road, Luton, LU2 7HA is the address.

Wardown Park in the spring is a gorgeous treat. The lake
reflects the brilliant blue sky, and the verdant surroundings
come to life. Enjoy a boat ride on the lake, take a leisurely
walk along the paths bordered with flowers, and soak in the
beauty of spring as it unfolds in this charming location.

Pro Tip: For a lovely day in nature, pack a picnic and
unwind on the verdant grounds.

Walled Garden at Luton Hoo (51.8425° N, 0.3769° W):
The address is LU1 3TQ, Luton Hoo Estate.

Visit Luton Hoo Walled Garden to discover a world of
horticultural delights. With trees and flowers in full bloom,
springtime provides a riot of color. Discover the well-kept
garden and savor the aroma of the spring flowers.
Workshops and seasonal activities are also held in the
garden.

Pro Tip: While you're there, see if there are any lessons on
flower arrangements and gardening.

2) **Summer Vacation Getaways**

Luton's summer welcomes you to enjoy the warmth of long, bright days. Here's how to enjoy the summer vibes in this bustling metropolis, from outdoor activities to cultural events.

Park Leagrave (51.9067° N, 0.4257° W):
Marsh Road, Luton, LU3 2NL is the address.

Come to Leagrave Park and enjoy the finest of summertime. The river's twisting path and vast grassy areas provide the ideal setting for outdoor events like picnics. Play a game of frisbee, go for a stroll along the riverbanks, or just unwind in the sun.

Pro Tip: Keep an eye out for summertime activities including park concerts held outside.

51.8830° N, 0.4161° W: **The Bear Club**

Mill Yard, 24A Guildford Street, Luton, LU1 2NR is the address.

Venture inside The Bear Club, Luton's summertime nightlife. Soulful performances bring this jazz and blues venue to life. Indulge in the lively ambiance of this little club while taking in live music and tasty refreshments.

Pro Tip: Look through their schedule of events to see unique concerts and summer jazz festivals.

The Luton International Carnival in Different Venues:
Info@lutoncarnival.co.uk via email

Attend the Luton International Carnival to celebrate Luton's diversity. This lively celebration, which takes place in the summer, includes dance performances, music, and colorful parades. Take part in the celebrations as various cultural rhythms fill the streets.

Pro Tip: Make reservations for lodging in advance and schedule your visit around the days of the carnival.

3) **Autumn Adventures**

Luton is covered in warm colors as fall approaches, making it a charming place to explore the outdoors and engage in cultural activities. With these fall time explorations, embrace the shifting of the seasons.

The golf course at Stockwood Park (51.8894° N, 0.4086° W):
London Road, Luton, LU1 4LX is the address.

Set out on the Stockwood Park Golf Centre among the breathtaking fall scenery. The 18-hole golf course has a picturesque, ever-changing color background. Experience the refreshing autumnal air while playing a game of golf, regardless of your level of skill.

Pro Tip: For a fruitful learning experience, make use of the coaching sessions offered by the golf facility.

Houghton Hall Park: Park Road North, Houghton Regis, LU5 5FU; Address: 51.9066° N, 0.4141° W

Houghton Hall Park turns into an autumn paradise. There is a lake, walking routes, and woodland sections in the large park. Take in the gorgeous scenery of the changing leaves as they turn from green to gold, making for a relaxing walk in the fall.

Pro Tip: Dinfo@lutonculture.comon't forget to pack a camera so you can document the breathtaking views of the lake and the changing foliage.

Luton Culture: located at 51.8780° N and 0.4146° W

Address: Multiple Sites

Take advantage of Luton Culture's events and exhibits to savor autumnal cultural pleasures. Discover the town's vibrant cultural scene as the leaves fall, from theatrical plays to art galleries. For the most recent fall schedules, see their website.

Pro Tip: For a more thorough cultural immersion, take part in guided tours or art workshops.

4) **Charms of the Winter**

Luton is magical throughout the winter months because of the holiday lights, warm gatherings, and celebrations of the season. Make the most of the holidays by exploring the town's winter marvels.

LUTON TRAVEL GUIDE 2024

51.8828° N, 0.4299° W, or the XC

Address: 34-38 Dallow Road, Luton, LU1 1TR, Junction 10 Business Park

At The XC, embrace the essence of winter. Indoor skiing and climbing are among the winter-themed activities available at this indoor leisure facility. The XC offers a getaway to a winter wonderland, perfect for thrill-seekers and families alike.

Pro Tip: See their calendar for courses and activities with a winter theme.

St George's Square Christmas Market (51.8790° N, 0.4175° W):
St George's Square, Luton, LU1 2AZ is the address.

During the Christmas market, St. George's Square is transformed into a joyous and enchanting place. Discover the quaint booths providing homemade crafts, seasonal delicacies, and unique presents. The festive mood and sparkling lights provide the ideal environment for Christmas shopping.

84

Pro Tip: To really enjoy the enchanting atmosphere of the market, schedule your visit during the evening.

Ice Skating at 51.8789° N, 0.4174° W at Luton on Ice: St George's Square, Luton, LU1 2AZ is the address. info@lutononice.com via email

Ice skating at Luton on Ice is a great way to welcome winter. Skaters of all ages are invited to use the makeshift ice rink located in St George's Square. Savor the excitement of ice skating in the center of Luton, together with the festive music and sparkling lights.

Pro Tip: Make reservations for your ice skating session in advance, particularly during busy holiday periods.

Luton's charm never goes out, and the town's character is enhanced by the changing of the seasons. Throughout the year, Luton extends a warm welcome to everyone, whether they are taking in the vibrant springtime hues, basking in the summertime warmth, discovering the picturesque fall scenery, or welcoming the joyous winter festivities. Consider the season while making travel plans, and allow the town to reveal its treasures at every turn of the year.

SPECIAL INTEREST TRAVEL

A. Wine Tours and Vineyard Visits

Take a voyage through the thriving vineyards of Luton, where each taste reveals a different tale and the vistas like a painting of undulating hills.

i. **The Stockwood Discovery Center Vineyard is located at 51.8843° N and 0.4044° W.**
London Road, Luton, LU1 4LX is the address.

Visit Stockwood Discovery Centre Vineyard to learn about the craft of winemaking. This vineyard, which is tucked away on Stockwood Park's grounds, provides guided tours that show you how grapes are grown. Savor samples of their regionally made wines, which include interesting Luton-only combinations.

Reservation: The Stockwood Discovery Center website allows you to make reservations for tours.

ii. **Vineyard Offley Hoo (51.8885° N, 0.3808° W)**
Offley Hoo, Hoo Lane, Offley, Hitchin, SG5 3DU is the address.

Experience wine sampling in a tranquil setting at Offley Hoo Vineyard. This vineyard, which is just a short drive from Luton, offers stunning views of the surrounding landscape. Learn about the winemaking process from the vine to the bottle by taking one of their guided tours.

Reservation: To schedule your wine tasting, send an email to Offley Hoo Vineyard.

iii) **The Winery & Brewery in Chiltern Valley (51.6892° N, 0.9471° W):**
Hambleden, Henley-on-Thames, RG9 6JW is the address.

Visit the Chiltern Valley Winery & Brewery, renowned for its fine wines and artisan brews, for a picturesque day excursion. See the wine production facilities, stroll through the vineyards, and end your tour with a tasting that highlights the variety of their several award-winning wines.

Reservation: Use their official website to make an online reservation for your tour and tasting.

B. Spa and Wellness Getaways

Relax and revive in the pleasant health havens of Luton, where contemporary spa treatments are combined with peace.

i. 51.8425° N, 0.3769° W: Luton Hoo Hotel, Golf & Spa
The address is LU1 3TQ, Luton Hoo Estate.

At the Luton Hoo Hotel, Golf & Spa, live in luxury. This graceful house has a top-notch spa retreat with steam rooms, indoor and outdoor pools, and a variety of restorative services. Encircled by gorgeous parkland, it's a peaceful haven.

Reservation: The Luton Hoo Hotel website allows guests to make reservations in advance for spa services and packages.

ii) Bannatyne Health Club & Spa: The location is 51.8766° N and 0.4196° W.
1 Regent Street, Luton, LU1 5FA is the address.

In the center of Luton, at Bannatyne Health Club & Spa, revitalize your senses. With cutting-edge amenities including a heated pool, sauna, and a range of wellness treatments, it's the perfect place to unwind for the day.

Reservation: Via the Bannatyne Health Club & Spa website, spa treatments, and day passes may be made online.

iii) **The Luton Wellness Centre, located at 51.8835° N and 0.4232° W:**
Address: LU1 1SA, Luton, 2 New Bedford Road

Visit the Luton Wellbeing Center to experience holistic wellbeing. Offering a variety of treatments to enhance both physical and emotional well-being, this institution provides everything from therapeutic massages to yoga and meditation workshops.

Reservation: For information about programs and appointments, get in touch with the Luton Wellness Centre directly.

C. Adventure Tourism

For those who like extreme sports, Luton's varied landscapes provide exhilarating experiences.

i. Canyoning and Rafting

White Water Center in Lee Valley (51.7726° N, 0.0179° W): Station Road, Waltham Cross, EN9 1AB is the address.

Water sports aficionados will find paradise at the Lee Valley White Water Centre, which is just a short drive from Luton. Savor the exhilaration of canyoning and white-water rafting in a safe and beautiful setting. For novices and experienced explorers alike, the facility offers professional guides.

Reservation: Make your reservations on the official website of the Lee Valley White Water Centre for your rafting or canyoning experience.

ii. Exploration and Caving

The Caves at Chislehurst (51.4066° N, 0.0571° E): Caveside Close, Old Hill, Chislehurst, BR7 5NL is the address.

Less than an hour's drive from Luton, Chislehurst Caves awaits you for an underground experience. These historic caverns provide guided tours down winding passageways that showcase WWII and prehistoric folklore stories.

Reservation: The Chislehurst Caves website allows guests to schedule tours in advance.

Hell-Fire Caves: Location: 51.6511° N, 0.9259° W Church Lane, West Wycombe, High Wycombe, HP14 3AH is the address.

Discover the enigmatic Hell-Fire Caves, renowned for its distinctive rock formations and fascinating history. Explore the caverns' depths to learn the Hell-Fire Club's secrets.

Reservation: On-site or online ticket sales for guided tours are available for Hell-Fire Caves.

Luton offers a wide range of unique interests, from wine tasting in verdant vineyards to relaxing in opulent spa getaways to seeking heart-pounding thrills. Create a custom schedule based on your interests and let Luton show you its many sides. This will guarantee an amazing trip that is unique to you.

LUTON ITINERARY

Greetings from an interactive tour of Luton's center! This itinerary has been thoughtfully designed to highlight Luton's abundant natural beauty, diverse experiences, and rich cultural heritage. Prepare to discover this energetic town, which offers a perfect balance of history, adventure, leisure, and delicious food.

Day 1. Explore Luton's History

Wardown Park and Museum in the morning (51.8777° N, 0.4179° W)
Old Bedford Road, Luton, LU2 7HA is the address.

Take a leisurely walk around the lovely Wardown Park to start your day. After taking in the tranquil surroundings, visit the Wardown Park Museum, which is situated in a Victorian home. Discover the history of Luton, from its lace-making heritage to the development of its culture.

Lunch at The Castle in the afternoon (51.8783° N, 0.4181° W)

98 Castle Street, Luton, LU1 3AL is the address.

Make your way to The Castle for a delicious meal. A menu of modernized British classics is available at this historic tavern. Savor regional cuisine and take in this little establishment's warm atmosphere.

Luton Hoo Estate in the evening (51.8425° N, 0.3769° W)

The address is LU1 3TQ, Luton Hoo Estate.

Visit the Luton Hoo Estate to round off your day. Discover the magnificent grounds and see the magnificence of the Luton Hoo Hotel. To ensure the ideal conclusion to your first day in Luton, think about indulging in a superb dinner experience at the hotel's restaurant.

Day 2: Culinary Pleasures and Cultural Immersion

Stockwood Discovery Centre in the morning (51.8843° N, 0.4044° W)

London Road, Luton, LU1 4LX is the address.

Explore the rich cultural tapestry of Luton by visiting the Stockwood Discovery Centre. Discover the winery, exhibits, and lovely gardens. Make the morning a morning of exploration by becoming involved with the town's art and history.

Lunch at The Bricklayers Arms in the afternoon
(51.8947° N, 0.3805° W)
38 High Street, Flamstead, St. Albans, AL3 8BZ is the address.

Visit The Bricklayers Arms, a quaint tavern in the adjacent hamlet of Flamstead, for a unique experience. Savor a classic pub meal in this elegant environment.

Evening: George Street's Culinary Adventure (51.8783° N, 0.4153° W)
George Street, Luton, LU1 2AA is the address.

George Street is a gourmet mecca with a wide variety of restaurants. Investigate neighborhood eateries and cafés while trying various cuisines. George Street has something for every taste, regardless of whether you're craving foreign cuisine or regional delicacies.

Day 3: Adventure, Nature, and Relaxation

Leagrave Park in the morning (51.9067° N, 0.4257° W)
Marsh Road, Luton, LU3 2NL is the address.

At Leagrave Park, where the natural world reigns supreme, start your day. Take a stroll in the morning, play outside games like frisbee, or just unwind along the riverbanks.

Adventure at the Lee Valley White Water Center in the afternoon (51.7726° N, 0.0179° W)
Station Road, Waltham Cross, EN9 1AB is the address.

Visit Lee Valley White Water Center for an exhilarating experience. Take part in exhilarating water activities like canyoning or white-water rafting. Professional guides provide an exciting and safe experience.

Bannatyne Health Club & Spa in the evening (51.8766° N, 0.4196° W)
1 Regent Street, Luton, LU1 5FA is the address.

Come to Bannatyne Health Club & Spa to relax and rejuvenate. Savor spa services, have a swim in the pool, or just unwind in the sauna. It's the ideal way to cap off an exciting day full of adventures.

Day 4: Shopping and Culinary Discovery

Luton Market in the morning (51.8787° N, 0.4145° W)
The Market Hall is located in Cheapside, Luton, LU1 2HT.

Experience the distinct local vibe at Luton Market. Look around the booths selling handcrafted handicrafts, fresh food, and other items. Interact with neighborhood merchants to get a taste of the lively market scene.

Lunch in St George's Square in the afternoon (51.8790° N, 0.4175° W)
St George's Square, Luton, LU1 2AZ is the address.

St George's Square is a chef's paradise with a wide variety of restaurants. Savor a leisurely meal while taking in this major square's vibrant ambiance.

Shopping in The Mall Luton in the evening (51.8781° N, 0.4148° W)
37 The Mall, Luton, LU1 2LJ is the address.

Finish your day at The Mall Luton with a little shopping therapy. Discover a variety of places to pick up one-of-a-kind mementos to bring back home, from specialist shops to fashion boutiques.

This four-day schedule offers a taste of Luton's many facets. Luton provides a wide range of experiences, from outdoor recreation and spa getaways to gastronomic discovery and cultural exploration. You are welcome to modify this schedule to suit your needs, and let Luton's kind welcome lead you on an unforgettable adventure.,

CONCLUSION

In summary, Luton emerges as an enthralling location that skillfully combines a rich past, vibrant culture, and a variety of activities. Every angle of the cultural tapestry of Stockwood Discovery Centre and the tranquil surroundings of Wardown Park conveys a different tale.

A tapestry of memorics is woven together by culinary explorations on George Street, heart-pounding excursions at Lee Valley White Water Centre, and peaceful moments at Luton Hoo Hotel & Spa. Luton's allure is undeniable, whether one chooses to indulge in spa getaways, embrace nature, or learn about the town's history.

The sounds of Luton's historical sites, the hospitality of its residents, and the tastes of its food stay long after you say goodbye to this vibrant town, making it a memorable part of your travel experiences.

FREQUENTLY ASKED QUESTION

Here are some frequently asked questions about Luton, along with informative answers:

Q: What is the best time to visit Luton?

A: The ideal time to visit Luton is during late spring to early autumn (May to September) when the weather is mild, and outdoor activities thrive. However, each season unveils unique charms.

Q: How can I get around Luton?

A: Luton boasts an efficient public transportation system, including buses and trains. Taxis and car rentals are also readily available, providing flexibility for exploring nearby attractions.

Q: Are there any hidden gems in Luton?

A: Absolutely! Explore the hidden gems in local neighborhoods, like the charming pubs in Flamstead or the lesser-known parks offering serene retreats.

Q: What are the must-try dishes in Luton?

A: Indulge in Luton's culinary delights with iconic dishes such as Luton Clanger, a savory-sweet pastry, and explore diverse international cuisines in the bustling dining scenes.

Q: Are there day trips available from Luton?

A: Yes, venture on day trips to nearby destinations like Houghton Regis or embark on guided tours for enriching experiences beyond Luton.

Q: How can I experience Luton's cultural scene?

A: Immerse yourself in Luton's culture by visiting museums, attending festivals, and exploring local markets. Engaging with the community and attending events will provide an authentic cultural experience.

These FAQs offer a glimpse into planning a memorable trip to Luton, ensuring a seamless and enriching travel experience.

Safe Travels!

Printed in Great Britain
by Amazon

55130689R00056